Sales Copy Pro
How to Write High Converting Sales Copy Every Time

Thomas H. Perrie

Copyright © 2017 Thomas Perrie

All rights reserved.

ISBN-10: 1542620538
ISBN-13: 978-1542620536

DEDICATION

This workbook is dedicated to every hard working man and woman who dared to dream outside the lines; and to my family, for never telling me that I was working too hard… even when I was.

CONTENTS

	The Importance of Sales Copy	Pg 1
1	The Headline	Pg 6
2	The Problem	Pg 10
3	The Only Real Solution	Pg 13
4	Your Qualifications	Pg 15
5	Your Solution	Pg 17
6	Social Proof	Pg 19
7	Make Your Offer	Pg 21
8	The Guarantee	Pg 23
9	Scarcity	Pg 25
10	Call To Action	Pg 26
11	The Warning	Pg 27
12	The Reminder	Pg 28
	Conclusions & Next Steps	Pg 29

THE IMPORTANCE OF SALES COPY

Generating sales online is, in a lot of ways, a numbers game. Driving traffic to a sales page and watch as a percentage of visitors convert into sales. The goal is to get the percentage of converts as high as possible, since in one way or another, the traffic is going to cost you – either in time or in a straight up financial sense.

The quality of the traffic that you send to your sales page is going to be the first key factor that you will want to consider. It is not directly the focus of this course, but it should go without saying that you want to try and target people who will be interested in your product or service when driving traffic to your site. The advent of social media has made this a whole lot easier for beginners and those without massive budgets.

The other key factor, which is the exact focus of this course, is the content of the sales page itself. What your sales page says has been proven (not that it needed to be proven, since its surely common sense) to have a huge impact on the conversion rate of visitors into buyers.

The difference between poorly crafted sales copy and professionally written copy is like night and day. Some people have a natural leaning towards the kind of thing that works, but almost no one is born with the innate knowledge of how to write sales copy that converts highly – it's never been part of our evolutionary past, so it makes sense that this is something that needs to be learned.

The Best Kept Secret in Sales Copy Writing

Many view copy writing as some sort of mystical black art, where the copywriter is some sort of magician that can work his or her magic over your business. Now, it may be true that a high converting sales page can utterly transform a business, but there is no magic to it.

Far from it.

Here is the thing that copy writing experts fo not want you to know: copy writing is a science, not an art... and certainly not magic.

It can be broken down, dissected, split apart and analyzed.

The very best sales copy can be taught. Not just memorizing and rehashing existing sales letters, but the principles; the underlying attitude and goal of each section can be replicated for any product or service. Each of these sections can be linked together to make sales copy that converts to an exceptional level.

By dividing up sales copy into a series of sections, and then analyzing those sections to understand the reason behind them and what they are attempting to do with the reader, it becomes easy for even inexperienced writers to create outstanding sales copy. All original, all your own work, but by following the section by section guidelines, you can be walked through the process of writing strong sales copy that converts exceptionally well. Even if you have never done it before.

Call it a template, a formula, or a process – you can call it whatever you want... but the fact is that we have it, and through this course, so will you. Once you learn it you will see it in every sales pitch you come across. You will start to notice when it's not done quite right and therefore could be improved. And most importantly, when you write your own sales pitches, you will be able to see massive results as you deliver the highest level of sales copy repeatedly.

Resistance is futile

Everyone has one reason or another to not buy from you, no matter what you are selling. They will have some reason to resist you. Now, that reason may not be very strong; it may be based on an error (such as they do not correctly understand what your product/service does); or it may be a huge obstacle. Everyone has an objection or a reason to resist a product – otherwise everyone would buy everything! Your role, as sale copy writer, is to handle the objection and overcome the resistance to purchase, whilst at the same time convincing them to act. It is the companies that can do this successfully that earn the most and get the sales. It's certainly not because they have the best product... what a wonderful world it would be if this were the case. No, it's the company that can best understand why people would not want to buy their product, and then find a way around that for the customer, that get the most sales.

Not all objections are verbalized by potential buyers. Many will keep their cards close to their chest, so to speak, and prefer not to comment on their reasons. And of course, many sales pitches are given in such a way that you do not ever hear from the potential customer about their reasons – this is truer today than ever before in human history, since the advent of the internet, there have been countless sales pitches delivered through non-personal media (like a web page) where the scope for feedback is very small. It is in these non-personal deliveries that preparation work of the sales pitch is so critical – because the only feedback you will get from the customer is whether they buy or not... and at that point it's too late to do anything about it.

Buying Motivators

There are lots of different reasons that push people into the act of buying, but they all basically fall into a handful of categories, or motivators as we call them.

This is not an exhaustive collection, but the basic motivators for potential buyers are:

They want to be wealthy
They want to be healthy/physically attractive
The want to have more free time
They want to have fun
They want security
They want some form of enlightenment or inner peace

Deep down this is what most buyers want, to one degree or another. Even buyers who operate on behalf of large companies fall into these categories – a company will generally only buy your product or service if it makes them money or saves them time. As a broad rule of thumb, the more of these buying motivators that you can satisfy, the more likely you are to make a sale.

It may not be immediately obvious that your product ticks one or more of these boxes, it is the job of your sales copy to spell these out for the potential buyer.

Buying Objections

You need to know your customer's objections and resistance points ahead of time if you are going to effectively combat against them throughout the sales copy. You need to have a solid grasp of what motivates a buyer and what holds someone back from making the leap with their wallet.

Here are some classic purchase objections that you might be struggling with in your business. Use these as a starting point to determine what your customers object to about your product or service.

"It's too expensive"
"You do not understand my problem"
"I don't trust that you know what you are talking about"
"What you propose will not work for me"

Remember we are still talking in general terms right now, we will get to writing your sales copy in the next few modules, but for now it's important for you to start thinking like your potential customer – what drives them, what holds them back?

Think about your product – what might a buyer's objection be? Is your product a high-ticket item? This need not be a bad thing, so long as you remember that the higher price will exclude a lot of potential customers.

Is your solution or service hard to explain properly? Maybe you deal in a complex industry, in which case you may need to invest some time in coming up with a simply way of explaining your product or service – a way that does not exclude those less knowledgeable in your chosen field.

A second rule of thumb about your sales copy is that the more of these objections that you successfully overcome, the more likely you are to make a sale.

Your sales copy should handle and cover these objections, thus leaving the buyer with no good reason not to buy your product… yes, it might be a high-ticket item, but I can easily make my money back by using the product for just a couple of weeks… or, yes it might be that the buyer felt you were not an expert in your field, but your sales copy makes it clear that you know exactly what you are talking about.

SECTION 1: THE HEADLINE

In many ways, the headline of your sales copy is the most important part. A poorly written headline will often be the only part of the sales copy to be read by potential buyers. In other words, if you get the headline wrong, the rest of what you write does not matter.

Depending on what you do with your sales copy, your headline can take different forms. Perhaps it will be the title of the sales email that you send. Or the header at the top of the letter you post. More likely it will be the title of your article or landing page. Whatever format you choose to use your sales copy, your headline has the exact same role: to get your reader to continue into the body of the sales copy.

We previously outlined what drives and hinders buyers from spending. Armed with that information, you may already be thinking smart about your headline. In case you are struggling to join those dots, here is what you need to do:

Find strong motivators for your potential buyers.

Finding a way to relieve fear is often the most powerful. What problem does your product or service solve? How awful would it be for your buyer to totally fail in this area? This is often the hook that you can use to reel in your target.

Of course, fear is not the only motivator. Rather than listing again the motivators from module 2, let me give you some sample headlines that you can use simply by filling in the blanks. Or just take them as examples and come up with your very own headline…

The "How to…" Headline

"How to _____ "

If your product or service solves a problem for you reader, then highlighting that you are about to instruct them on how to solve said problem is a naturally strong way to go with your headline. However, stronger still would be:

"How to _____ in order to avoid _____"

Do you see how we take the same instructional headline but inject an element of fear? You can even throw in adjectives to make the fear even more powerful

"how to _____ in order to avoid the nightmare of _____"

Emphasizing the fear really dials it up a notch. It is possible to overdo this however, so I would not dial up the fear much beyond this!

The "Secrets of…" Headline

Another powerful headline tactic is to use a mystery angle to entice the reader to continue into your sales copy. A simple headline, like the example below can be very effective:

"secrets of _____ revealed"

Of course, this is not the only way you can use mystery. Almost any turn of phrase that implies most people do not know what you are about to tell them can work wonders. Another twist on this would be to introduce an element of fear into the headline. So you might want to adapt your headline to read:

"Never before taught method for _____ could save your business thousands"

The idea that a business could hemorrhage thousands is enough to panic most small to medium business owners. Do you see how the mystery is included with the "never before taught" phrase, and fear introduced with the "could save you thousands". This is quite a subtle fear line, however, so you may even want to beef it up a little with something like:

"You are risking the future of your business if you do not implement this top-secret method for _____ in the next __ months"

Whereas the previous example was a subtle implication that not reading on might cost you money, this headline uses fear to really grab the attention of the reader, then introducing mystery.

The "warning" headline

A warning headline can be a greatly effective tool for getting people to stop what they are doing and read on into your letter. This can be particularly effective if you are using your headline in a social media situation (say, a Facebook advert) since people suffer from a kind of blindness when it comes to what they are looking over as they scroll down the page. The warning headline can be used to jar their mind and cause them to pause, almost on instinct. Of course, it can also be effective in other situations too.

The most obvious warning headline looks something like this:

"Warning: If you are a business owner then you need to read this now!"
If you are selecting colors then you could even print the "warning" text in red, the rest in black, just to make it really stand out.

But this is not the only warning headline

"Stop what you are doing – this is MUST HAVE information for _____"

You can apply the warning headline with any other motivator that you want, but as we have discussed, fear is the strongest of human motivators.

"Warning: Businesses will fail without implementing _____ in the next ___ months"

Non-Business to Business Headlines

All the examples given here have been related to business to business transactions, but I hope that you realize that these can be tweaked and repurposed to any subject matter you like – they are essentially universal principles for selling to the human race.

"Warning: You are never going to get your dream girl without this top-secret trick"

"Top secret method for dog training revealed"

Remember the purpose of the headline

When you craft your headline, you need to keep in mind the goal. Yes, it needs to in some way represent the content that you include in the following copy. But there is a greater goal – to create a desire; a need for the reader to continue. The more you can create this in your readers, the more successful you will be.

Leverage motivators, but tailor them to your product or service. Your headline should not try to attract everyone, just as your copy should not attempt to appeal to everyone. You need to know who you are trying to target and speak to them – speak to their desires, their fears and their aspirations. Ultimately your headline needs to create a single thought in the head of the reader:

That you do not know what the solution is, but you know what you need to do – read on!

2 THE PROBLEM

Where the headline gets the reader's attention, this first section needs to demonstrate to the reader that they have not made a mistake in stopping to read your copy. By far the best way to do this is to outline the problem that your product or service solves.

To do this you need to think about why someone would buy what you are selling. What does it the problem look like? What does it feel like to have that problem? These are what you want to outline in this section. You want your target buyer to read this section and to absolutely relate to the problem you are outlining. A sentence or two showing that you understand some of the pain that your buyer feels will make them much more likely to trust and buy from you.

Sales letters that perform OK will stop there. But great sales letters will push it just a little further. What you need to do next is agitate the problem in the mind of the buyer. By this I mean really drive home, almost exaggerate the scale and severity of the problem – not to a comedic level, but just enough to make the customer emotionally react to your copy. I do not mean like a noticeable physical reaction like tears, but the slight overstatement of how the problem feels will cause the reader to connect with what you are saying.

This is the difference between good and great sales letters. This is the extra mile, one of the secrets that the big name copy writers do not tell you.

What might this look like?

The exact detail of what the passage will look like will depend a lot on what you are offering. And to whom you are offering it. Let me give you an example passage to get your thought processes flowing:

"does it not just drive you crazy when people visit your website and leave within just a few seconds? I mean really, what could they have seen in the blink of an eye that would cause them to suddenly close your site? You spend time and money on driving traffic to your site – hours on social media, fortunes on advertising or search engine optimization... Money you could have spent on refining your service, hiring new staff, or even just taking your family on vacation. And all you have to show for it is a couple of seconds and not a buyer in site. If this is you then I know how you feel. I have been there too."

You can see from the example that we jump straight in to the problem. This grabs the attention of the reader, particularly if they can relate to the situation you outline. Therefore, it is so important to know who it is you are targeting. Your product is unlikely to appeal to everyone. Indeed, most products will only ever appeal to a small percentage of the available population. So, you need to know what group is likely to be interested in your product. And really go after them. Remember that a sales pitch general enough to appeal to everyone is unlikely to have strong enough appeal to get anyone to buy.

So, we hit them with the problem, and the only people who we are interested in are the people that can relate to that problem, since that is the problem your product or service solves. So, what do we do? We drive it home. We rub salt in the wound of the problem that our target reader faces – we linger on it, dwell on, in this example we remind them about all the other ways they could use the money they are wasting on junk traffic. This is the step that brings our sales copy to life making it stand out I terms of the successful conversions that it will bring.

The personal touch: In It Together

But then we do something else. We have not touched on it yet, although it's in the example.... Did you spot it? We make it personal. It's not just their problem. Not any more, now it's our problem... I am with you, I feel your pain, I have been there. This implication of solidarity is pure sales gold. There are numerous ways in which you can slip this in, so long as you make it personal.

> Trust me
> I know what you are going through,
> I have felt that pain
> When I was in that position it nearly killed me

These are all powerful phrases that you can use to make it personal. This creates a subtle yet powerful emotional connection: The reader (assuming he can relate to the scenario that you outlined) will inherently trust you more, and accept what you say a little more readily when this is done right. And that can make all the difference in terms of conversion rates.

3 THE ONLY REAL SOLUTION

In this section of your sales copy, we are going to present your reader with your solution to the problem that you have just outlined. Thus, far you have managed to play on the customer's negative experiences and emotions to get them to listen and connect with you. Now that you have proven yourself to be someone who understands where the customer is coming from, you have a certain amount of authority to demonstrate your solution.

But we do not want to jump right on into that. No, first we want to highlight to them the other solutions that are available. Of course, you do not want to paint them in a positive light. You should point out that there are other solutions, but that these solutions are bad – then explain the reasons. Let me give you an example.

"Of course, there are business coaches who can show you how to manage your social media profiles, but even the cheapest business coach can cost thousands of dollars each month – and do you really even want to trust your business with the *cheapest* business coach that you can find?"

Do you see how we take a solution to a problem and present it to the reader in such a way as to ensure that the reader does not consider it a viable option? It's such an easy thing to do and it has multiple benefits: Such statements actively push your competitors out of the mindset of the reader, whilst simultaneously strengthening your own authority position in the readers mind, because everything that you say, that the reader knows to be true builds up your credibility in their mind. It makes them trust you more because you have said more that they agree with and know to be true.

You must make sure that you do not insult your competition, or say anything that a prospective buyer might disagree with. Your downplaying of the opposition must be done using niggles and doubts that are on the customers mind already, or at least be thoughts that our virtual reader will find easily believable. An easy way to do that is to take a perceived strength of your opposition and use it as a weakness. The reader (assuming they know the opposition you are talking about) will recognize the strength that you bring up and will either already have the niggle about them, or because they see the truth of that fact, are ripe for believing and accepting the doubt that you are planting. Let me give you some examples:

Your competition is a massive multinational and you are a small startup: "do you really think that a multinational company can treat you like q valued customer? How can they, when you are just a number to them? Your business needs one on one care, the kind that a faceless corporation just cannot provide. "

Your product is more expensive than some of your competition: "you and your business deserve q type end, world class solution to this problem. Putting the success of your company in the hands of the lowest bidder is a recipe for financial ruin."

I am sure that you get the idea.

4 YOUR QUALIFICATIONS

If you have been writing along and following the guidelines from this workbook, then you will have already crafted a sales letter powerful enough to have your reader on your side, creating a sense of gratitude in your target readers – gratitude that they may have just stumbled upon something that will make a real difference for them. Never underestimate the power of this emotional response, it is the ability to manipulate and control this response that separates truly outstanding sales copy from your bog-standard sales copy. These differences can make or break the fortunes of businesses.

Now you want to dazzle your reader with reasons to listen to you, rather than anyone else. Remember that they are on your side – they like you, they know you can relate to them and you understand their struggles. You have shown them how other solutions to their problems will not work, and then you hit them with your own solution which will (naturally) deliver the results that they so desperately need.

So, you introduce yourself – what you and/or your company do. Give them evidence that you know what you are talking about – tell them how long you have been working in the industry, how successful you have been and maybe some of the people you have worked with or for (so long as you think they will have heard of them). No one wants to hear your resume, you need to keep things relevant to what you are selling. Here is an example of this section in action:

"Hi, my name is Joe Smith, and I have been working in social media for the last 8 years. In that time, I have worked with some of the biggest names in the automobile industry and have successfully managed and grown social media accounts in various platforms with a combined following of 300 million people! Suffice to say, I know the social media landscape for business. I have grown accounts, managed account and leveraged accounts for Ford, Lexus, and BMW to name just a few. I am known in the automobile industry as the go to guy for social media management."

No mention of academic achievements, although there are sometimes where this can be beneficial (see below) but rather we are keeping on message. We know the target reader that we are looking for and we keep going out of our way to press their buttons and exclude everyone else. In the example above, we are clearly targeting business owners/executives within the automobile industry with a social media related problem. We may capture the attention of those in linked industries, or even the occasional random business owner, but in this example, we know that our primary business is the automobile industry, so we shamelessly target them – we want to speak to them over anyone else. As should you, with your target audience. There are a hundred different ways you could present yourself, so choose to do so with your target audience in mind. Make everything you say relate to them.

You can include, if relevant:

People you have worked with
Events you have been part of
Awards or achievements

You get the idea…

5 YOUR SOLUTION

At this point you can now introduce your solution to the very specific problem you have been highlighting. This, you will have noticed, is the first mention you have made of your product. That's bot a mistake. Thus, far you have been warming up the reader, using subtle techniques to influence their reaction to you. It's been subtle, but statistically it's significant. Your reader is now ready to hear about your product. So, introduce it:

"It's because I understand the pain that this situation can cause, that I have spent the last 18 months developing and fine tuning the ultimate solution. Let me introduce you to Product X."

This is the perfect opportunity for you to talk about your product. Although you need to be careful here. Remember that the reader doesn't care about your product. They care about their problem and are looking for a way to ease that problem. Presenting the wonderful attributes of your product will alienate your reader. What you need to do is dazzle them with the benefits of owning and using your product, rather than a list of attributes your product has.

If you imagine product X to be a service that grows businesses social media following with targeted followers, then the attribute would be:

"product x had the ability to increase your social media following."

Now, you may think that's a good sales line, and certainly there are a number of people who would read that and be educated enough in business to know why that would be a benefit. But b not presenting the benefit, you are alienating everyone else who is not able to join those dots. A much better Line would be

"product x works 24/7 hunting down fresh leads for your business day after day. You would never run out of targeted leads who were interested in your service"

It's the same thing, only the latter is spun to highlight the benefit of the attribute not just display the attribute itself. This can massively influence your conversion rate.

there is a practical exercise you can do to help you go from a list of attributes to a list of benefits. Write down all the positive attributes of your product or service. Now take them one at a time and spun them from a benefit perspective. This is the kind of copy that converts like gangbusters.

When you write this section of your sales copy you should seriously consider bullet pointing these points. You want them to stand out so even if the reader is quickly scanning the text rather than reading, these points will jump out.

Also, remember to list all the benefits. Often a customer will buy a product or service based on a single benefit that particularly speaks to their issue or situation.

Insert chapter six text here. Insert chapter six text here. Insert chapter six text here. Insert chapter six text here. Insert chapter six text here. Insert chapter six text here. Insert chapter six text here. Insert chapter six text here. Insert chapter six text here. Insert chapter six text here. Insert chapter six text here. Insert chapter six text here.

6 SOCIAL PROOF

By this stage in your sales copy, you will almost certainly have the reader wanting to believe you. However, some people take more convincing than others. Social proof can be a very powerful convincer for the human psyche.

Social proof works on two different levels. The first is that it just flat out makes you more believable.

The second level that social proof works on is that humans hate to be the first to do something. If they can see proof that others have gone ahead first, then your buyer is much more likely to go ahead. Seeing quotes and testimonials from real people will make everyone more comfortable with a purchase.

I know in this skeptical world many of us take those testimonials with a pinch of salt, but even the more skeptical amongst us will be more inclined to o purchase if they are included. It's a statistical fact.

What social proof looks like

When we talk about social proof, I am talking about personal endorsements or positive reviews by people who have used the product or service before.

Not all social proof converts the same. The more human you can make the social proof, the more effective it will be. Here are the variations or social proof formats, in order from least to most effective.

A quote
A quote with a photo
A video testimonial.

As I said, the more human you can make a testimonial the better. And nothing online is as human as a person looking into camera and stating that your product or service has benefitted them.

Something else that can really lend credibility to your social proof is if you include contact information from the reviewer. Most people will never use them, but the fact that they are included makes the social proof all the more compelling. This can be extremely powerful.

7 MAKE YOUR OFFER

This is a key stage in your sales copy. If your offer is terrible, then even the best sales copy will not benefit you that much. Of course, you may gain an additional sale here or there but the adage is ultimately true: that great sales copy can transform a mediocre offer, but even the very best sales copy cannot save a whale of an offer.

Clearly, your offer will depend largely on your business so by the time of writing sales copy, it may be too late to impact it in a significant way. The best we can do in this section is to help you understand what a great offer looks like.

A high converting offer should be a 'no brainer' for your target reader. You appeal directly to a pain point they have and present them with an attractively worded solution. When they see the price, the best reaction that you can hope for is "I would be a fool not to jump on this!".

All too often I see outstanding sales copy, that has me desperate for the product but when the price and offer is announced its totally disproportionate to the issue. Just because you can charge a million dollars for your service, does not mean that you should charge a million dollars for your product. Charging more for your product does not always equate to earning more... If only life were that straightforward. I do not mean to imply that you should aim low with your pricing, but keep in mind your target audience and the severity of the problem you are offering to solve for them. A high converting offer should, as I have said, be an overwhelmingly obvious choice for the targeted reader: you highlight a problem he has, remind him of how bad it is and how it affects him, then you swoop in with a product that totally resolves his issue. He can afford the product and its price is proportionate to the size and scale of the problem being resolved. Such a customer would be crazy not to jump on the product. But if you were offering a $100 product for a $5 problem, then you may still make sales, but not nearly as many.

More than a price

Your offer is likely more than just a price tag, however. A great offer would also include incentivized terms and/or extras. Common examples of incentivized terms would be offering a monthly payment option for a higher ticket item, or perhaps 0% interest.

Extras do not always need to cost you money. Access to free training videos on how to use your product for example, can go a long way both in terms of creating value and in alleviating a fear in the mind of a potential buyer – a fear that they will not be able to get to grips with your product. Extras should be tied into your product in some way – having them should make sense and benefit your product. Offering a free garbage disposal with every social media training program just would not make any sense, for example.

You can justify a higher price by increasing the value of your offer. For lots of reasons this is advantageous, just so long as you remember the guidelines previously stated – that the price needs to be in proportion to the problem being solved, and within the reach of your target demographic.

There is no set formula for this. To price optimally, it requires that you are familiar with your audience both in terms of what they can afford and how much pain the problem that you are addressing causes.

8 THE GUARENTEE

Online purchasing requires a certain amount of faith on the part of the buyer – often they will not know you, and as such almost certainly not inherently trust you. These days everyone is aware of the online scammer - who will bolt as soon as they take your money. No matter how professional your website, how well-crafted your sales copy, there will always be a niggle of doubt the first time someone purchases from you. Your sales copy thus far has taken steps to address that - by presenting you as an authority in your field, someone who understands the pain that the buyer feels. Of course, the social proof goes a long way to help, especially if you have been able to include contact details for those leaving feedback. But you should now go an extra step and confirm without any doubt that unsatisfied customers will be able to get their money back.

I know some people will instinctively worry about this – won't this be abused by someone who gets the information I am providing and then gets their money back. But the essential point is this – abuse of returns and refunds policies is a lot less common than you would imagine.

As it happens, almost every business has a returns policy, whether they publicize it or not – if you had a very unhappy customer who bought your product but felt mislead or let down then you would refund them... so why not increase buyer confidence by announcing this upfront?

Your guarantee does not need to be anything fancy, but it does need to be clear that you will be happy to refund anyone less than 100% happy with your product, no questions asked. Of course, you can embellish this, beyond the usual 30 days. Some people will offer 60 days' refund period. Others will offer longer or even a 150% percent refund:

"If you are genuinely not happy with the service I offer – if you follow the steps and it does not increase your conversions, I will gladly offer you not just 100% of your money back, but I will give you 50% extra back, on top of a full refund as an apology for failing you!"

You get the idea – make it clear, make it emphatic and try and personalize it if you can. Boldness and confidence at this point will have a massive impact on your readers confidence in you.

People will often struggle to believe a deal if they feel it's too good to be true. So, if your guarantee is outrageously high, then you need to say something about why it is, and why you feel you can be so bold:

"I have worked with hundreds of businesses and have been able to positively influence their profit levels through my coaching. I have never had a business I could not benefit and I have no intention for your business to be the first! If my coaching does not have a positive impact on your profit margins – a trackable, demonstrable positive impact, then I will give you 150% of your money back. I have never needed to do this before, and I have no intention of letting you or anyone else down."

9 SCARCITY

This is a very simple idea, which is equally simple to put into practice... yet so easy to get wrong. Let me explain:

Fear of missing out can be a very powerful motivator for the human condition. If you have presented an offer that genuinely appeals and excites your reader, then letting them know if they do not take action that they might miss out can be the final straw in getting them to take action.

Scarcity can take a couple of forms. It can either be a limited time deal, or a limited quantity deal:

"we only open our coaching program to 15 businesses at a time, so we can ensure they get the support and attention that they deserve. This offer is based on a first come, first served basis, and when we close the doors, it will be another 12 months before we open them again. Buy now to avoid disappointment."

You see, it's not a complicated thing. But yet it can be badly misused. If you make a statement about limited offers, you need to live up to that statement. If you do not, then you will massively erode trust and shatter any relationship moving forward. Your business – any business – relies on repeat custom, on a strong reputation. If you lie and deceive your customers then they will not come back, and for the sake of pushing a single sale, you risk losing a customer for life.

So, learn this lesson ahead of time – do not make promises that you cannot keep.

10 CALL TO ACTION

Never assume that your reader will know what to do next, should they want to take you up on your offer. You may have a massive "BUY NOW" button, but if you assume the reader knows what to do, you will be alienating a whole group of people. I know it sounds insane, but you need to spell this stuff out. Doing so will not put off someone who knows what to do (so there will be no negative to including a clear call to action), but by including it you will increase the number of sales you get (a clear advantage to including it)

This does not need to be a big deal, just a clear instruction for how the reader should progress in order to be a customer. If there are additional steps beyond buying now, then you can outline them too. Taking the mystery out of the purchase will help increase the sales conversion rates.

"Just click the buy now button below to take advantage of this limited time offer. Once payment is made you will be taken directly to a download page where you can access your coaching program instantly."

It's simple, it need not be more than a couple of sentences, but it can make a significant difference in terms of your conversion rates.

11 THE WARNING

Outstanding sales copy will never stop building emotion and moving the reader along. Even at this stage in the copy, after the benefits and scarcity have been outlined, you can still add to the emotion in the mind of the reader by reminding them of what they are going back to if they choose not to make a purchase from you. This, in a way, mirrors what was covered at the start of the sales copy. Do you remember when you highlighted the problem that the customer faces and you over-emphasized the pain that they feel because of it? This section has the same idea in mind. Hammer home the problem again. In a sense, you are reminding them of what they are choosing to lose by not buying from you.

Your aim is to paint them a picture that they are already familiar with – the problem, the pain, the struggle. They have the solution in the palm of their hands, yet without action they will lose it and return to the daily hardship of living with the problem.

This is the opposite of listing the benefits. Feel free to use bullet points here too. Think in terms of specific pain points that the customer will feel without your solution:

Too much effort for too few clients
Struggling to manage your workload
Not able to have the kind of free time that you want
Financial hardship, struggling to make ends meet

I am sure you get the idea; your list will be dependent on the nature of the product/service that you offer.

12 THE REMINDER

You want to end your sales copy with a final reminder. Make it bold and stand out. The easiest way to do this with written copy is with a PostScript (a PS.) This will make it jump out to the reader, especially if they are scrolling down quickly to see the price etc. Because of this trend in scrolling down quickly (it's annoying but a percentage of your readers will do this, then based on the price will either read the rest of the copy, or even just jump in and buy) your postscript will be one of the most read portions of your copy. It's crazy, but it's true, so you want to make sure that your PS really sings.

There are a couple of things that you should include:

A reminder of your amazing offer
your key selling points (the main benefits to the reader),
Your scarcity claim
A clear call to action (where to click)

This sounds like a crazy simple step, but it really does get noticed. Many copy writers will miss this out, but in doing so they are missing a valuable opportunity to reiterate the message and get it out to the reader.

CONCLUSIONS AND NEXT STEPS

If you have been following along with this workbook then you will now have a fully formed sales letter. Exactly what you do with this is entirely at your own discretion. But whether it becomes the script for a video or a sales page on your web site it will serve you well and consistently convert readers into buyers and subscribers.

Being able to write compelling sales copy will put you at a massive advantage to your competition, who will either need to make do with average text, or pay a small fortune for a professional sales copy writer. In short, you are now the man or woman to beat. And there is little else that neither you nor I can ask for, than that.

ABOUT THE AUTHOR

Thomas Perrie has been working for almost a decade in the online marketing space, after completing his honors degree in Media and Film. Thomas is a passionate entrepreneur, who relishes the challenge of working with brick and mortar businesses and aspiring independent authors to help them thrive online.

www.ingramcontent.com/pod-product-compliance
Lightning Source LLC
Chambersburg PA
CBHW061235180526
45170CB00003B/1303